Grade I Piano Sol

16 enjoyable pieces for Grade 1

CW00495218

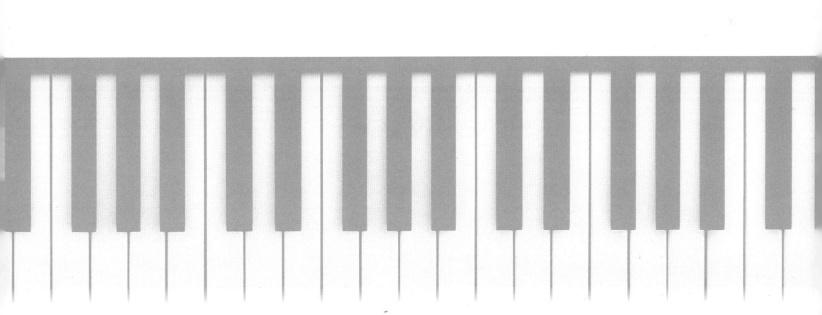

Published by

Chester Music
part of The Music Sales Group
14-15 Berners Street, London W1T 3LJ, UK.

Exclusive Distributors:
Music Sales Limited
Distribution Centre, Newmarket Road,
Bury St Edmunds, Suffolk IP33 3YB, UK.

Music Sales Pty Limited
Level 4, Lisgar House,
30-32 Carrington Street,
Sydney, NSW 2000 Australia.

Order No. CH83622
ISBN 978-1-78305-972-0
This book © Copyright 2015 Chester Music Limited.
All Rights Reserved.

Edited by Toby Knowles.
Arranged by Alistair Watson.
Music processed by Paul Ewers Music Design.

Printed in the EU.

Your Guarantee of Quality
As publishers, we strive to produce every book to the
highest commercial standards.
This book has been carefully designed to minimise awkward
page turns and to make playing from it a real pleasure.
Particular care has been given to specifying acid-free, neutral-sized paper
made from pulps which have not been elemental chlorine bleached.
This pulp is from farmed sustainable forests and was
produced with special regard for the environment.
Throughout, the printing and binding have been planned to
ensure a sturdy, attractive publication which should give years of enjoyment.
If your copy fails to meet our high standards,
please inform us and we will gladly replace it.

www.musicsales.com

Grade 1 Piano Solos

16 enjoyable pieces for Grade 1 pianists

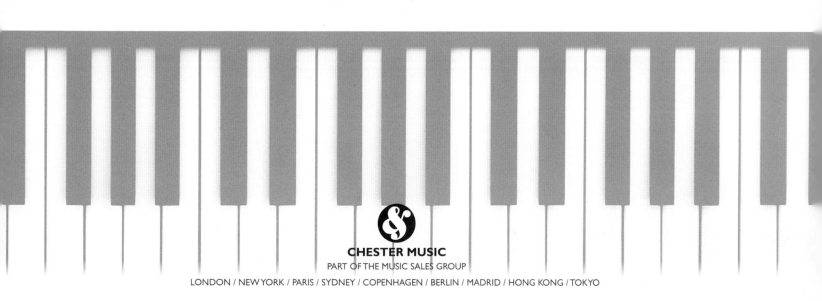

CHESTER MUSIC
PART OF THE MUSIC SALES GROUP

LONDON / NEW YORK / PARIS / SYDNEY / COPENHAGEN / BERLIN / MADRID / HONG KONG / TOKYO

Contents

Amazing Grace

Traditional
Words by John Newton

Play this piece slowly, with even triplets.
There are four long phrases—try to keep each one legato in the right hand.

The Can Can

Music by Jacques Offenbach

Notice the change of key at bar 19—practise an F major scale before starting.
Your right hand wrist will need to be very relaxed to play the staccato notes.

Bright and upbeat (♩ = 90)

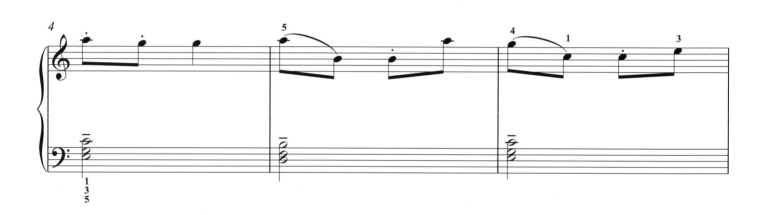

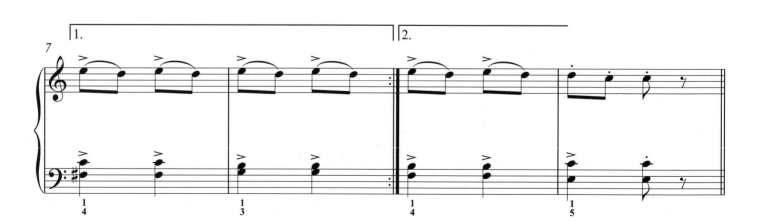

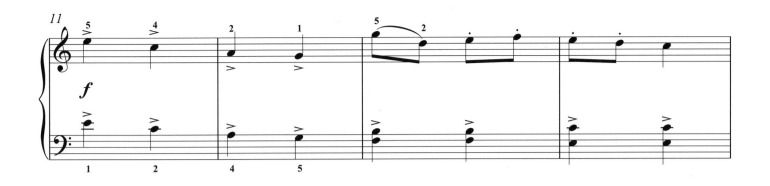

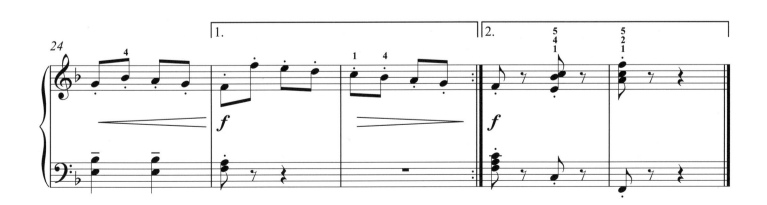

Can You Feel The Love Tonight

(from Walt Disney Pictures' *The Lion King*)

Words by Tim Rice, Music by Elton John

Let the melody of the verse flow freely, like a conversation.
The verse can be played gently, but play much louder (forte) in the chorus.

In free time (♩ = c. 100)

Slow down

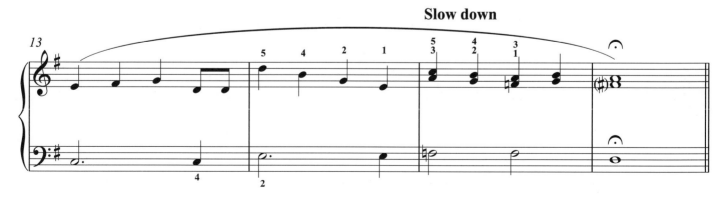

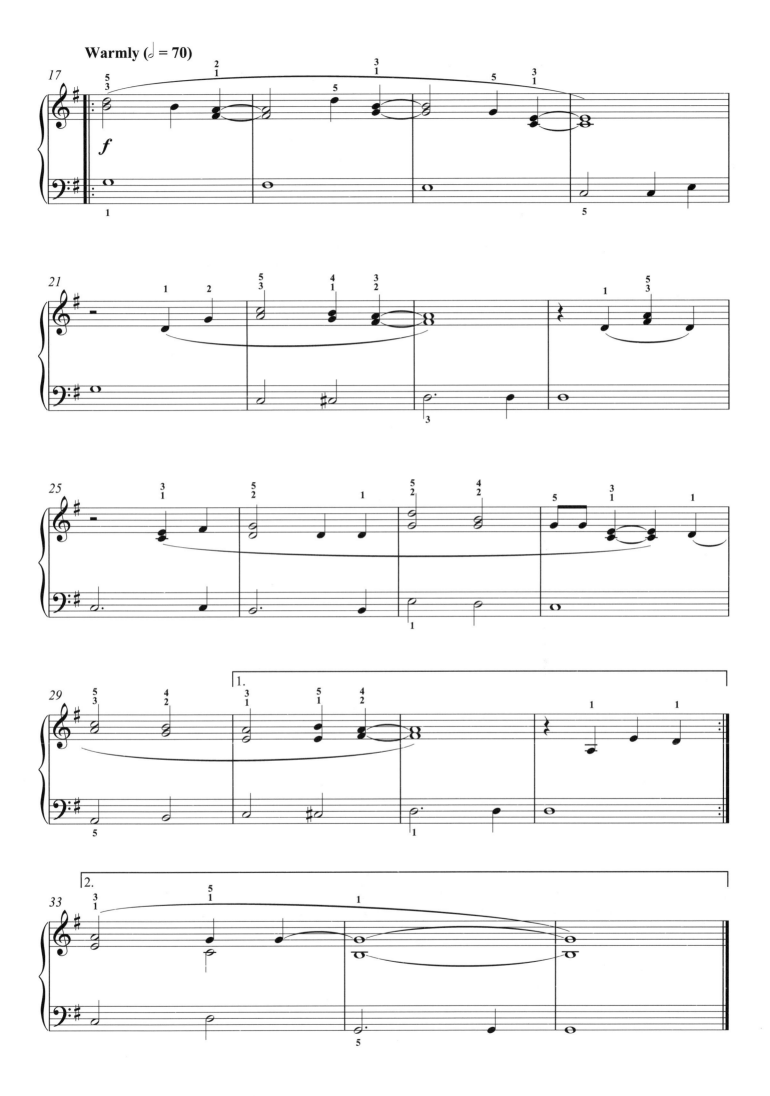

Counting Stars

Words & Music by Ryan Tedder

Try to play the right hand melody *cantabile*—in a singing style.
Don't start this too fast—watch out for the right-hand semiquavers in bar 15.

Steadily (♩ = 80)

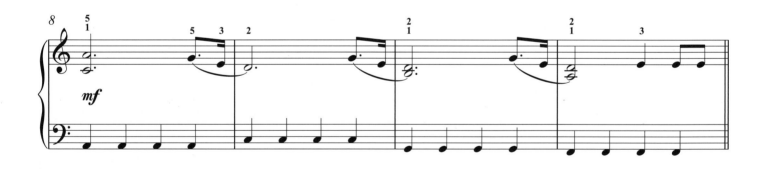

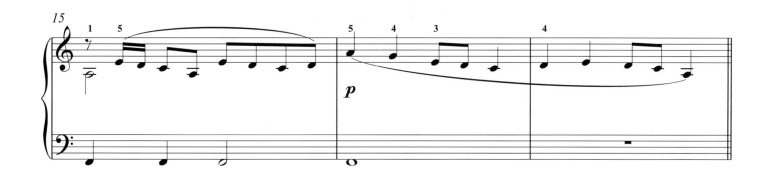

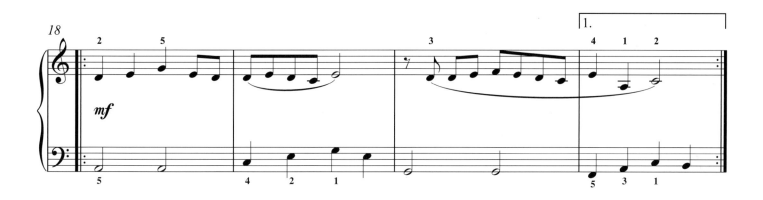

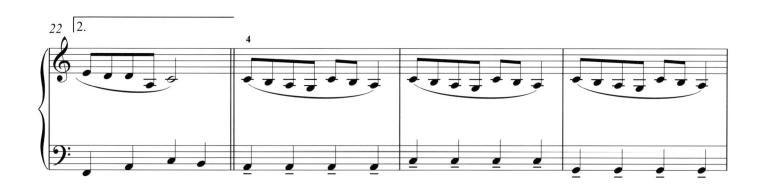

rall or rit
Slow down

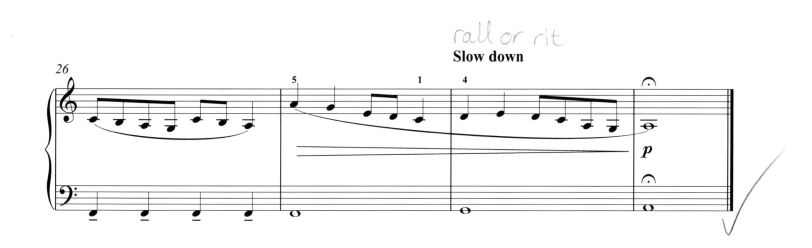

Do You Want To Build A Snowman?

Words & Music by Robert Lopez & Kristen Anderson

This piece should be played delicately. The melody line is made up of short phrases with rests in between.
Make sure you count carefully during the rests.

Moderately, expressive (♩ = 100)

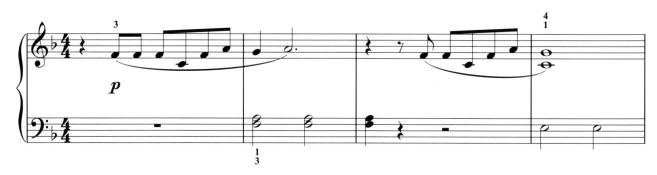

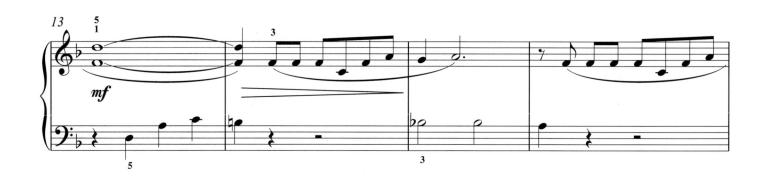

Slower

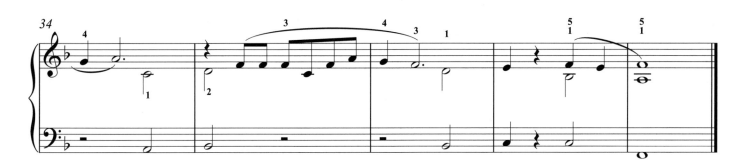

How Long Will I Love You

Words & Music by Mike Scott

This is a gentle song: play it very delicately. The 2/4 bar is easier than it looks—listening to Ellie Goulding's recording of this song will help you understand the rhythm better.

Gently (♩ = 60)

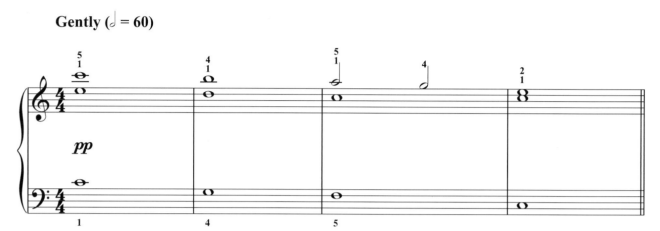

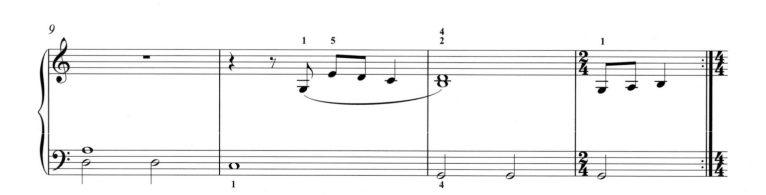

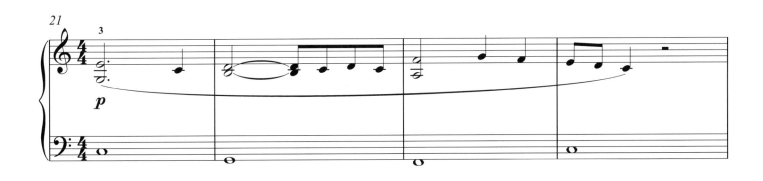

Slow (♩ = c. **46**)

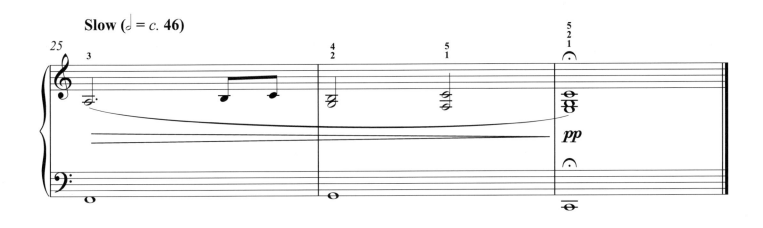

Let Her Go

Words & Music by Michael Rosenberg

Be careful not to rush the right-hand quavers.
The left hand often plays two notes—make sure they sound together each time.

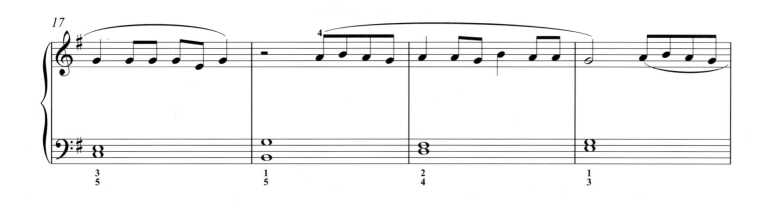

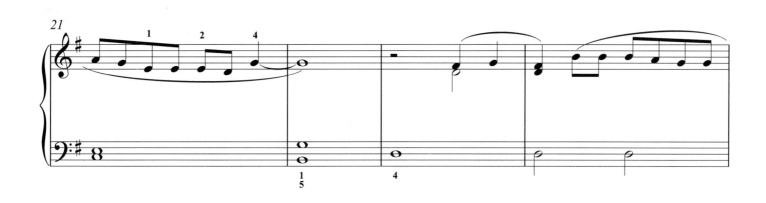

Slow down

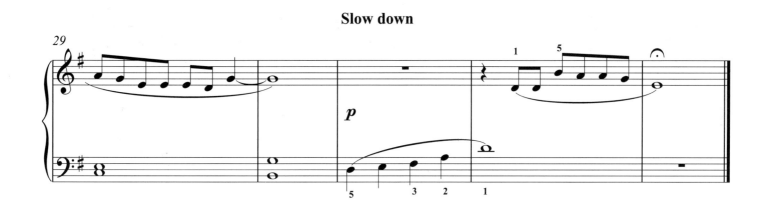

Let It Be

Words & Music by John Lennon & Paul McCartney

In this classic song the right hand gently plays the melody while the left hand keeps time.

Solemnly (♩ = 63)

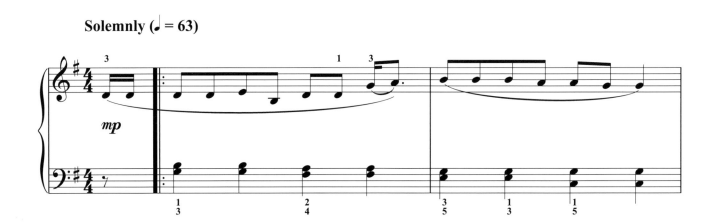

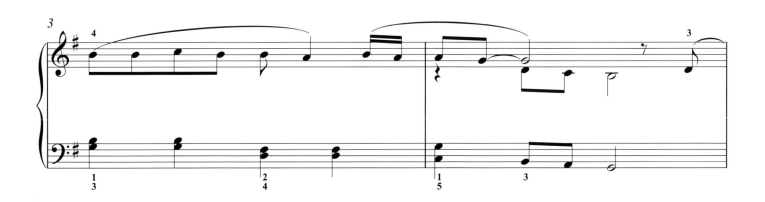

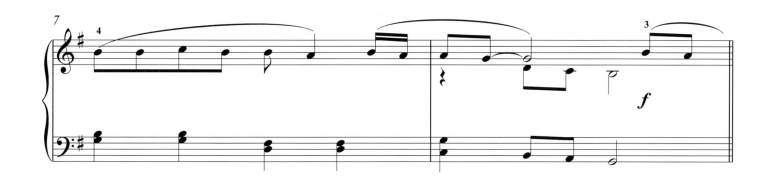

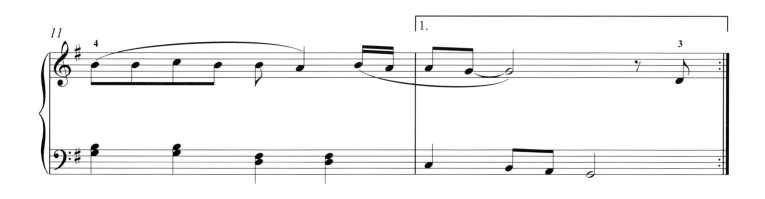

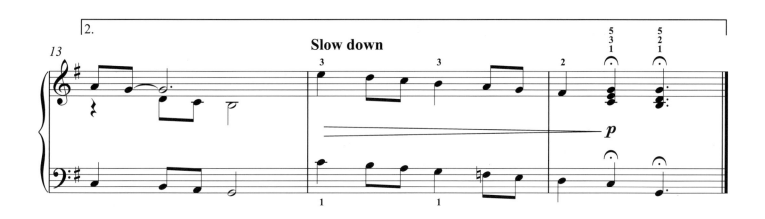

Lean On Me

Words & Music by Bill Withers

There are some tricky off-beats that need attention in this song.
Make sure you keep a strong pulse. Drive the song forward with the groups of four quavers.

Mad World

Words & Music by Roland Orzabal

This song needs a steady pulse. Play it quietly, as this will help convey the dark mood.
Be careful with the right hand rhythm in bars 2–4.

'O Sole Mio

Words by Giovanni Capurro
Music by Eduardo Di Capua

Let the music flow freely—you can take plenty of time over the pauses.
Build up to a dramatic climax at the end.
Practise the interval of a 6th with your right hand before playing the piece through.

Ode To Joy

Ludwig Van Beethoven

This should sound like a triumphant march. Play it loudly, but keep a steady tempo.
This is good practice for playing 3rds in the right hand. Try to make them sound legato.

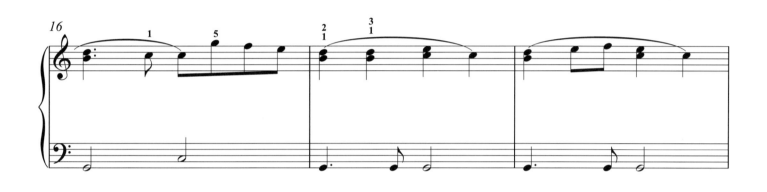

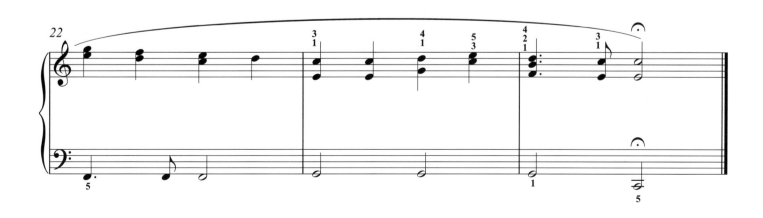

(Sittin' On) The Dock Of The Bay

Words & Music by Otis Redding & Steve Cropper

This is a relaxed and carefree song. Keep the left hand rolling along and never
let it sound rushed. Aim for crisp staccato notes in the right hand in the last two lines.

Peacefully (♩ = 90)

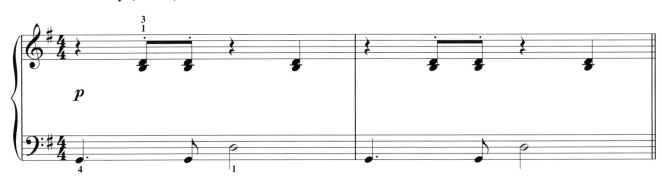

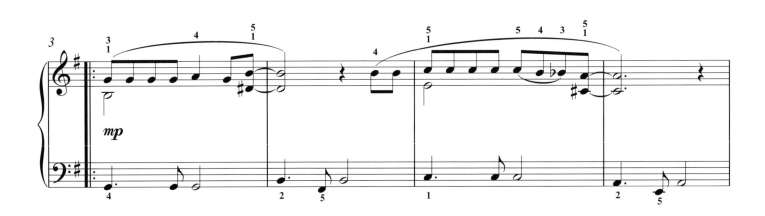

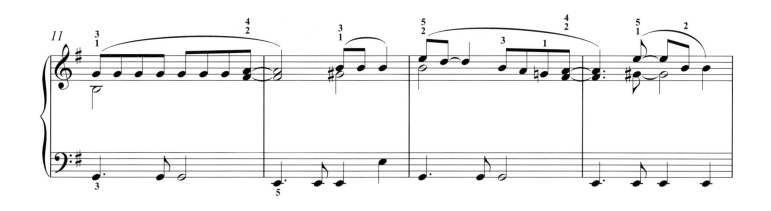

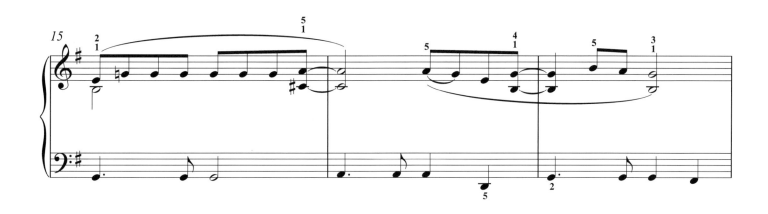

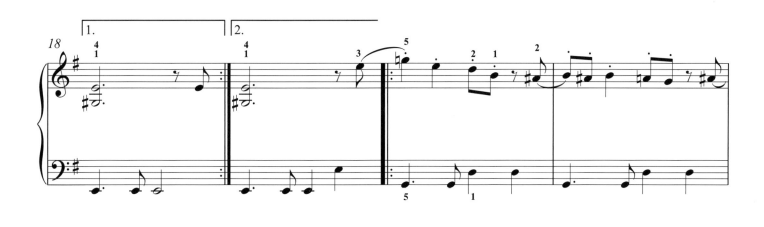

Skyfall
(from the Motion Picture *Skyfall*)

Words & Music by Adele Adkins & Paul Epworth

This song has plenty of drama—start softly and work up to a loud chorus.
Watch out for the tricky dotted rhythms in bar 20.

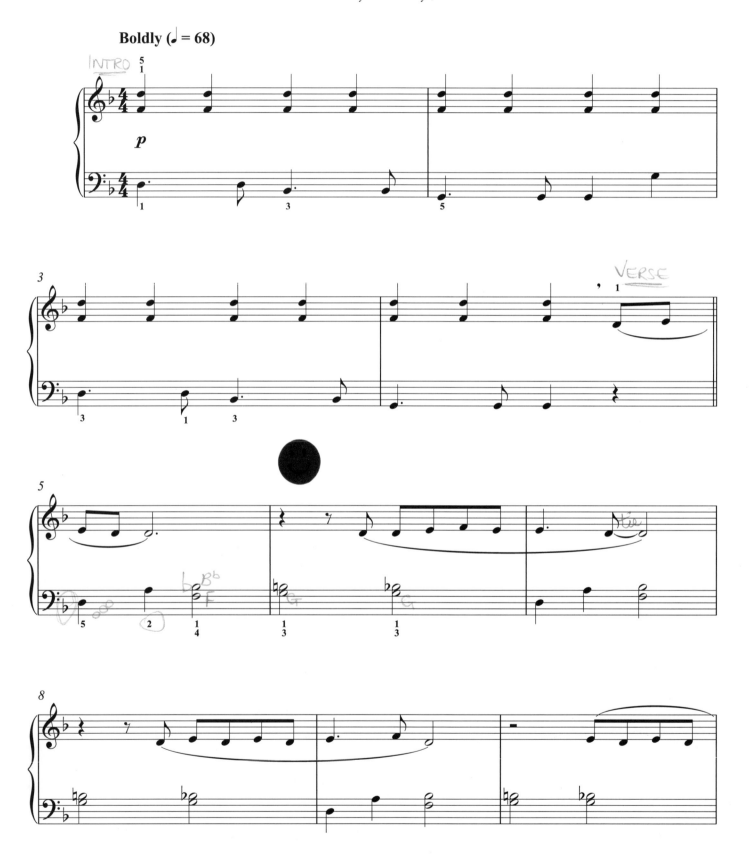

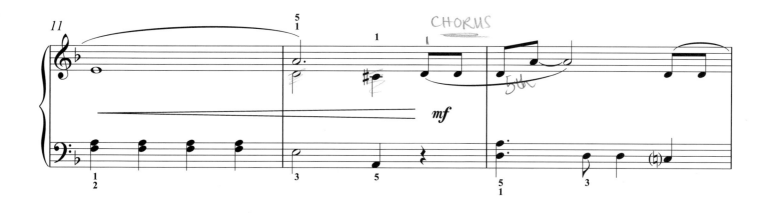

CHORUS

Slow down

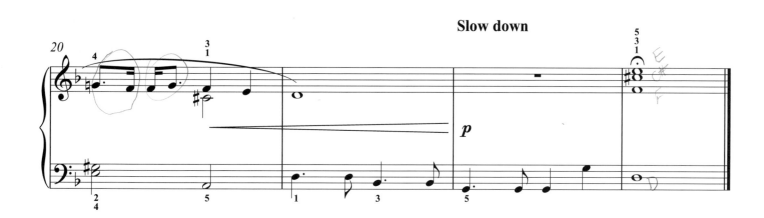

Scene from *Swan Lake*

Pyotr Ilyich Tchaikovsky

This melody is played by an oboe in the orchestra and should be played legato:
picture swans gliding gracefully over the water. Start softly and build up to forte in bar 12.

Swing Low, Sweet Chariot

Traditional

This is an old spiritual. Make sure you let the music 'breathe' between phrases.
Notice the B♭ in the key signature. There are some bars, however, where you play B♮.

1 2 3 4 5 6 7 8 9

Graded Piano Solos

The 16 pieces in these books have been specially arranged to provide enjoyable supplementary repertoire for pianists. Each piece has been adapted to fit within the specifications of the major exam board grades, and each book covers a wide range of styles, from classical and jazz pieces to contemporary pop.

Grade 1 Piano Solos

Including:
Amazing Grace; Lean On Me;
Do You Want To Build A Snowman?

CH83622

Grade 2 Piano Solos

Including:
All Of Me; Eine Kleine
Nachtmusik; Let It Go

CH83633

Grade 3 Piano Solos

Including:
Für Elise; The Snow Prelude No. 3;
Someone Like You

CH83644

Grade 4 Piano Solos

Including:
Air On The G String; Make You
Feel My Love; Summertime

CH83655

Grade 5 Piano Solos

Including:
Bridge Over Troubled Water;
I Giorni; Take Five

CH83666

AI

CW00494057

BLUE
SAXOPHONE

James Rae

UE 19765a

ISMN 979-0-008-03907-2
UPC 8-03452-01069-2
ISBN 978-3-7024-1326-2

www.**u**niversal**e**dition.com

vienna · london · new york

ALTO
SAXOPHONE

Mr Creek

JAMES RAE

Driving Rock tempo
(even quavers)

Universal Edition UE 19765a

Vintage Blue

JAMES RAE

Waltz for Emily

JAMES RAE

In the Wee Small Hours

JAMES RAE

Rachel and the Boys

JAMES RAE

JAZZY SERIES

18826	P. HARVEY/J. SANDS	JAZZY CLARINET 1
19361	P. HARVEY	JAZZY CLARINET 2
18827	J. RAE	JAZZY SAXOPHONE 1
19362	J. RAE	JAZZY SAXOPHONE 2
19393	J. RAE	JAZZY TRUMPET 1
18825	J. REEMAN	JAZZY FLUTE 1
19360	J. REEMAN	JAZZY FLUTE 2
18824	J. REEMAN	JAZZY PIANO 1
19363	B. BONSOR/G. RUSSELL-SMITH	JAZZY PIANO 2
18828	G. RUSSELL-SMITH	JAZZY RECORDER 1
19364	B. BONSOR	JAZZY RECORDER 2
19431	M. RADANOVICS	JAZZY VIOLIN 1
19757	M. RADANOVICS	JAZZY VIOLIN 2
16553	M. RADANOVICS	JAZZY CELLO 1
19711	T. DRUMMOND	JAZZY GUITAR 1
19429	J. RAE	JAZZY DUETS FOR FLUTES
19430	J. RAE	JAZZY DUETS FOR CLARINETS
19395	J. RAE	JAZZY DUETS FOR SAXOPHONE
19396	J. RAE	JAZZY DUETS FOR FLUTE and CLARINET
19756	M. CORNICK	JAZZY DUETS FOR PIANO
16536	M. CORNICK	JAZZY DUETS FOR PIANO 2
16537	M. RADANOVICS	JAZZY DUETS FOR VIOLIN

CHRISTMAS JAZZ

19184	J. RAE	CHRISTMASJAZZ FOR FLUTE
19186	J. RAE	CHRISTMASJAZZ FOR TRUMPET
19187	J. RAE	CHRISTMASJAZZ FOR CLARINET
19188	J. RAE	CHRISTMASJAZZ FOR ALTO SAXOPHONE
19189	J. RAE	CHRISTMASJAZZ FOR CELLO
19190	J. RAE	CHRISTMASJAZZ FOR TROMBONE
19185	J. RAE	CHRISTMASJAZZ FOR VIOLIN

www.universaledition.com

vienna · london · new york

BLUE
SAXOPHONE

James Rae

www.universaledition.com

vienna · london · new york

UE 19765b

ISMN 979-0-008-03907-2
UPC 8-03452-01069-2
ISBN 978-3-7024-1326-2

TENOR SAXOPHONE

Mr Creek

JAMES RAE

Universal Edition UE 19765b

Vintage Blue

JAMES RAE

Waltz for Emily

JAMES RAE

In the Wee Small Hours

JAMES RAE

Rachel and the Boys

JAMES RAE

JAZZY SERIES

18826	P. HARVEY/J. SANDS	JAZZY CLARINET 1
19361	P. HARVEY	JAZZY CLARINET 2
18827	J. RAE	JAZZY SAXOPHONE 1
19362	J. RAE	JAZZY SAXOPHONE 2
19393	J. RAE	JAZZY TRUMPET 1
18825	J. REEMAN	JAZZY FLUTE 1
19360	J. REEMAN	JAZZY FLUTE 2
18824	J. REEMAN	JAZZY PIANO 1
19363	B. BONSOR/G. RUSSELL-SMITH	JAZZY PIANO 2
18828	G. RUSSELL-SMITH	JAZZY RECORDER 1
19364	B. BONSOR	JAZZY RECORDER 2
19431	M. RADANOVICS	JAZZY VIOLIN 1
19757	M. RADANOVICS	JAZZY VIOLIN 2
16553	M. RADANOVICS	JAZZY CELLO 1
19711	T. DRUMMOND	JAZZY GUITAR 1
19429	J. RAE	JAZZY DUETS FOR FLUTES
19430	J. RAE	JAZZY DUETS FOR CLARINETS
19395	J. RAE	JAZZY DUETS FOR SAXOPHONE
19396	J. RAE	JAZZY DUETS FOR FLUTE and CLARINET
19756	M. CORNICK	JAZZY DUETS FOR PIANO
16536	M. CORNICK	JAZZY DUETS FOR PIANO 2
16537	M. RADANOVICS	JAZZY DUETS FOR VIOLIN

CHRISTMAS JAZZ

19184	J. RAE	CHRISTMASJAZZ FOR FLUTE
19186	J. RAE	CHRISTMASJAZZ FOR TRUMPET
19187	J. RAE	CHRISTMASJAZZ FOR CLARINET
19188	J. RAE	CHRISTMASJAZZ FOR ALTO SAXOPHONE
19189	J. RAE	CHRISTMASJAZZ FOR CELLO
19190	J. RAE	CHRISTMASJAZZ FOR TROMBONE
19185	J. RAE	CHRISTMASJAZZ FOR VIOLIN

www.universaledition.com

vienna · london · new york

BLUE
SAXOPHONE

James Rae

UE 19765

ISMN 979-0-008-03907-2
UPC 8-03452-01069-2
ISBN 978-3-7024-1326-2

www.universaledition.com

vienna · london · new york

PREFACE

BLUE SAXOPHONE has been composed with the aim of introducing saxophonists to music in the blues idiom. The pieces are of moderate length and in varied styles. The accompaniments have been written in such a way as to encourage the correct interpretation of the music.

Basic chord symbols have been added to the middle section of each piece to allow freedom for improvisation. Parts have been included for both B-flat and E-flat saxophones.

For ease of rehearsal, the saxophone part appears at concert pitch above the accompaniment.

VORWORT

Der Band BLUE SAXOPHONE wurde geschrieben, um Saxophonisten mit der musikalischen Welt des Blues vertraut zu machen. Die Stücke sind nur mäßig lang und decken verschiedene Stilrichtungen ab. Die Begleitung soll die richtige Interpretation der Musik fördern.

Einfache Akkordsymbole wurden in den Mittelteil jedes Stückes eingefügt, um dem Spieler die Möglichkeit zu freier Improvisation zu geben. Der Band enthält Stimmen für Saxophon in B und Saxophon in Es.

Für Probenzwecke wurde die Saxophonstimme in originaler Tonhöhe über der Begleitung gedruckt.

CONTENTS

Mr Creek

JAMES RAE

Universal Edition UE 19 765

Vintage Blue

JAMES RAE

Waltz for Emily

JAMES RAE

10

In the Wee Small Hours

JAMES RAE

Rachel and the Boys

JAMES RAE